Theseus
And
I
Eleanor Alder

Theseus And I
Copyright © 2023 Eleanor Alder
DARK THIRTY POETRY PUBLISHING
ISBN: 978-1-7397975-6-0

All Rights Reserved

Eleanor Alder
First edition

Artwork by Lisette-Elouise Powell

DTPP8

DARK THIRTY POETRY PUBLISHING

Circe's Spell On Glaucus

I hope you say my name in your sleep.
I hope it breaks in your throat
like glass,
that it chokes you.
I hope it makes it
almost impossible to breathe,
so, you wake startled,
panting like a dog.
With hair slick
against your forehead,
chapped lips, shivering.
I hope you discover a
gut wrenching sob
hiding beneath your tongue,
that it shocks you as it
slips free,
you didn't expect to wake
so suddenly
thinking of me.

I hope you say my name in your sleep,
a breathy whisper
caught between the sheets
—like a dream catcher.
Slippery palms
fisting the pillows.

Hot. Your body burns like
my fiery hair.
I hope that raging orange
flickers through your
flammable dream.
Spreading. Scorching.
The sneaking smoke
wraps around your throat
just enough to
coax forward a
gentle moan.
Your body softens in the places you
want it to be hard,
hardens in the places you
need it to be soft.
It wakes you up.
You are a fish out of water,
gulping down air.
Mind whirling from the
vivid flashes
 –soft curves and
parted mouths.
Your pray no one heard you,
no one can find out.

I hope you say my name in your sleep.
That it drips from
your lips like honey,
tugs gentle at the corners.

You take trips to the
late night theatre,
hidden in the
back room of your mind.
I hope you meet me there,
acting out the good days
–sweet memories and
gentle intimacy
that can't satisfy the
miserable hunger
spreading inside.
Fingers twitching,
sneaking over to the right side,
seeking out a familiar warmth.
It's the cold you find that wakes you up.
Stomach, a punching bag for panic,
realising what you have done.

I hope you say my name in your sleep,
and I hope you begin to find yourself
itching to taste the letters
on your tongue
while you're awake.

Forget The Poisoned Apple

You fed me promises, like raspberries,
until my stomach exhaled, content.
The red juice
stuck to my lips and
my lips clung to my cheeks, forming a smile.
I used my tongue to scoop the seeds
from my teeth and
they planted themselves in my stomach.
Sprung quickly, entwining with the other residents,
who long ago took root there. Traversed
the maze of organs and veins,
snuck through the bars
of the cage that held my heart. They bloomed
in terrible white, like the face of Thanatos.
Your sweet berries were laced with lies
and now bindweed twists through my body,
strangling the sunflowers and roses,
tulips and freesia. They all gasp for air.
Fall limp in a tight, final embrace.
This weed coils around my heart and constricts
like a thin, green snake.

Was He Embraced By King Midas?

He hid a bomb under my bed. Set it like an alarm clock to get us up in the morning. Tucked it under his side after I flicked off the light, used its soft ticking as a lullaby to lure him into a gentle sleep. When the day crept in, his alarm clock pushed at the bricks of my house until the whole building crumbled. The smoke from my singed hair clawed up my nose, clung to my throat and behind the shrill ringing, I found his muffled voice. His lips calmly forming words I couldn't quite hear. And when the glass rained over us prettily, like diamonds, tearing at my paper skin, it simply bounced off his body —as if he was sculpted from gold.

It's Not A Pirate's Life

I want it to be like a
storm striding in.
You feel the subtle shift in wind,
the waves below begin
to swoop quicker, deeper.
A cruel chill creeps
across your body,
starts at your arms,
slithers down your chest,
slips inside.

Flung to the deck,
body colliding with
rough wood, hard enough to
splinter your bones.
Your ship tilts
almost vertical, and you
dig your nails into the timber,
damp and slippery from the
downpour. Teeth bared,
jaw tight,
eyes watering.

I want this to be a shipwreck,
atop black, jagged rocks.
Drowning over and

over, washed up, bloated
and breathless.
Everything you thought was
treasure drags across the
ocean floor,
flaking gold paint and
Pound Shop glitter
melt away, caught up in the
current with the
wreckage and pain and
that is what I want this to be like.

He Gave Hermes A Run For His Money

One morning I woke up and he was packing a
suitcase.
I asked him what he was doing, and he told me
he had a flight to catch,
I shook my head
because I didn't realise he had a holiday booked, I
hadn't seen flight tickets or
a hotel booking confirmation,
he didn't tell me he was going away.

When he was on his way
out the bedroom door,
I told him to wait for me.
That I would come too.
If I wasn't going with him then I could
at least hold his hand on the way to the airport,
wave goodbye at the security gate.

But when I came stumbling
down the stairs, pulling on a
jumper, the same colour as his eyes,
he had already gone. Left
the door wide open and
forgot his keys.
I sent him a text that I loved him,
to let me know he got there safe.
He told me he had to put his phone

on flight mode. It has been on flight mode ever since.

Confessions From The Phantom Hearted

My hands ache from trying to
distract myself in the pages of a book.
I can't keep pretending I don't miss you.
I will never apologise for the memories
we share or the lyrics we poorly sang.
When I think about time, I think of
how quickly it passes. We are
not together anymore. Silence hangs
between us. I bought a sweater the
other day, the same colour as
your eyes.

Sources:
Courtney Peppernell, *Pillow Thoughts II: Healing the Heart* (Missouri: Andrews McMeel Publishing, 2018)

I Should Have Arranged A Visit With The Oracle

He poured wine into my eyes.
Everything I could see was stained by grapes.
I was drunk on his declarations, his passions
and obsessions, they
sat heavy in my stomach.

When he asked to stay an extra night
I thought that perhaps he was
hungry for more of my time,
became certain when I woke in the morning
and he had migrated to my side.
His nose pressed against the back of my neck.
Eyelashes caressed the skin,
arms knotted around me.
He was like a limpet
clung to a rock.

I wish had bought him a mood ring.
Then, I could have glanced down
at the hand grasping at the curve of my hip
that morning,
as he murmured at me to *come here.*
I could have sought out the
tiny crystal ball
hovering above his finger,
and found it was gravel grey.

And when he slid a piece of
carefully folded paper
across the coffee shop table,
etched the words of a love story
across the blue lines,
I could have
snuck a look at the plastic
painted silver, coiled around his finger
and realised that a story was all it was.

Ariadne

Theseus left me on this island but he will come back.
Before he left, he tucked me into his chest, and
rested his chin on my head.
I remember
feeling his heart hammering against my cheek,
trying to reach me, trying so hard
it left a pink mark on cloudy skin.
He wound my hair around his fingers
and scratched
I love you's into my scalp.
At night, I run my finger
over the marks his nails left behind.
He will come back.

I stood on the beach as he boarded his boat.
Watched through pooling eyes as he
drifted away from me and this island.
I had always believed quicksand to be a myth
but I was sinking into the ground,
the grains chewed at my knees.
The island was trying to swallow me up
because he was not looking back at me
as I stared out to him, with blotched cheeks.
So my mind pushed forward the memories
of him and me as we plotted the way
through the labyrinth. His fingertips
tiptoeing across my back,
breath fanning across my neck as

I revealed my plan. And
I held on to that
as his ship sank into the setting sun.
He will come back.

When it had been half a week
alone on this island,
I called out to the gods and they
let me send him a message whispered in the wind.
I told him I missed him. That I was sorry that
I made him want
                                    space.
I didn't tell him about the
                                    silence.
Or about the conversation I had with the
worm I found in my apple.
I counted the steps from one side of the
island, to the other,
while I waited for his response.
That night, I took a
crumpled up piece of papyrus
with me into my dreams.
It read: everything will be alright.

Theseus left me on this island, but he will come back.
The gods refused to send any more messages but
I have all the proof I need and it's not so quiet now.
The island is filled with a steady humming and
I have made friends with some vultures,
they sing to me
and kiss at my feet.

I noticed my fingers have stained black
but I think its just the berries, I let the
flies come and
lap at the juice.
In gratitude they tell me they have seen
Theseus, that
he is heading right for this island
and the promises he once
stitched into my lips
burn and I know it must be true.
He will   come back.
He will   come back.
He will   come back.

Were They Plastic Pennies, Or Do Wishes Just Not Come True Anymore?

My heart is playing tug of war
and you are the rope. One side
clings to the person that I knew,
the other digs its nails into the
person you now seem to be.
I want to just stop thinking of you.
I want to toss you, like a
penny down a well.
The wish that never came true.
No one ever remembers the wish
they made on a penny.
If I could just forget about you I wouldn't
risk my heart ripping in two.

I Invoke Mnemosyne

Once, everything between us was a wild forest.
It was swarms of bluebells,
butterflies and bees,
trees so tall they could be
ladders to the clouds, now
you can't even look at me.
You run to the other end of the train
to avoid being close to me,
as if I have a contagious disease.
When you walk my way,
you look straight through me.
I am a ghost,
wondering if I exist,
if we ever actually existed,
was the last three years nothing but a dream?

You boxed me up quickly.
Pushed me under your bed,
to collect dust with the rest of your history:
Captain America comics
and figurines, folders of A-level papers,
photo albums,
and now, me.
My limbs begin to stiffen
in agony from being
stuffed into such a meagre space.

There is no room for me down here.
My skin begins to grey
without the shine of the sun's rays.

Now, all there is between us is
                                        space.

Silence, echoing
                                                    b a c k

and
                        forth,
as we stand, trapped at traffic lights,
a meter   apart,
when before we would hold hands,
pressed shoulder to shoulder.
Instead, your jaw is tight,
eyes frozen on the destination straight ahead.
The flowers and grass that gathered around our feet
now
cling like the brown slush
that grasps at the sides of roads
when it has snowed.
Everything between us is
rot and decay and
I don't know
if that will change.

My Instagram Ghost

When I am not the ghost, you are.
Since the moment you ran,
you have been haunting me.
You follow me around, like a wasp,
I can't quite shake.
I wait,
try swatting you away,
disappear for a moment, but then,
back in my face.
I haven't seen you in weeks,
since before I bagged up everything I could find
that held a piece of you inside,
hid it all away,
still, you found a way to stay.

Before, Instagram was a
neglected friend, you would visit
every now and then.
Now, it is your favourite tool
to sting me with.
Reposting awful, dead memes,
rifle through your life to find anything,
anything decent enough to post on your story—
like you need it.
Like a smoker *needs* cigarettes, are you
addicted to proving you're right?

I had enough of tormenting myself with the
excessive life updates, I didn't ask for;
so I stopped watching your stories.
I left them, lingering like cobwebs
at the top of my screen.
Pushed you to the side.
Felt you slowly slipping from my mind—
forgetting that wasps are relentless.
Your perpetual buzzing rings down my ears again,
couldn't reach to
poke at my ribs from your place
on the ceiling of my phone screen.
Relocate to the top of my feed,
so you can stuff the
pages from your journal into my mouth,
I choke on your fresh memories,
your beaming face.
You've made your point now.
I get it, you're
happy without me.
You're such a happy, happy

        ghost.

Was The Icing Buttercream?

It is April and it is warm. I am surprised because April is an overfilled photo album for us. Your birthday came and went. You are twenty now. I did not cry. But I did wonder if you were thinking of me that day. I wondered if you looked at your cake, filled with candles and imagined in its place the cake I baked for you last year. I wondered if you glanced around your room that night at the gifts, I had previously given you for your birthday and felt something tighten around your heart. Like ribbons winding around wrapping paper, knotting into place. Now it is mid-April and the sun is still shining. Our would-be-anniversary is creeping in, so I check the weather forecast. It tells me that rain is coming.

I guess there could still be April showers yet.

Dealing With A Breakup When You Have OCD

I am a dog chasing its tail.
I run in circles, following
what is dangling in front of me.
When I finally sink my teeth in,
I realise it was only myself.

A thought opens a door into
a tight, dark room. The door closes behind me
and locks and there is no way out.

I find myself obsessing,
over-analysing every action I took,
everything I said in
the entirety of our relationship.
I feel guilty for things I don't know if I need to
feel guilty about. My fingers twitch to type
an apology just in case that thought is right
because how do I tell the difference
between an intrusive thought and when
I am in the wrong?

Now when my eyes burn
it's from the fear of what I could have done
rather than losing you. My tongue
throbs, desperate to ask
the question
I bite down on it hard,

before it can escape.

Cinnamon Summer Night

I wanted it to be special, so I swept my eyes with glitter, pulled a tiny skirt over bare thighs; it bit me in the ass a bit, because on the top of the hill, the evening's coastal chill gnawed at my legs, leaving behind little lumps, like mosquito bites. *We could leave if you like?* I shook my head. I wanted this. Stomach's full of Italian food, I leaned closer to you. Wrapped my arms around your shivering body, what's mine was yours, have my warmth. Your lips tasted of chocolate and wine, what was yours, was mine, you kissed me while we waited for the sun set. Whispered *sweet nothings* into my ear. Made me tip my head back, laugh so loud, the seagulls wouldn't stick around; took off into the darkening sky with a furious, squawking cry while the sun melted into the ocean, like a scoop of banana ice cream. Its reflection dribbled across the waves; above us, the sky exploded, we were sat inside of a flame, and I wanted nothing more than to remain in that slow, cinnamon summer night, forever.

Sometimes I Miss The People You Brought Into My Life, And That Is Okay

I saw your mum yesterday. I was on the bus and it drove past her, I noticed her hair was lighter, blonder and I had to trap my hands between my thighs and the seat to stop myself from jamming my thumb into the red stop button, stumbling off the bus just to tell her that her new hair looks beautiful, the last time I saw her, she told me not to leave it too long and now it has been five months, and I didn't realise how much I miss her, or how much I'm going to miss watching Love Island with her, or seeing her smile widen at the sight of chocolate, I wanted to ask her how she was, but I knew I couldn't do that. So, I let the bus pass her by. I took a breath. And then another. I still missed her, but I was okay.

Charon's Pennies

Your name has rusted on my tongue.
I spit
copper flecks when I speak
like embers
from our dying fire.
The heat
Blisters the fragile flesh of
my lips.
Soft skin bubbles and
pops, oozes
a metallic tang, like melted coins
that hardens
between my teeth.
Tumbles down
my coin slot throat until
I'm gagging
on your name
because it
just doesn't taste good anymore.

Acknowledgments

I would like to say thank you to Adam for seeing potential in me and my work. A massive thank you to Lisette for designing this gorgeous cover for me. Thank you to both Jack and Ruth for always believing in me and encouraging me. Thank you to everyone from my contemporary poetry class whose feedback helped develop this collection. Thank you to my Mum, to Georgia and to everyone who I both have and have not already mentioned for just listening to me when I needed someone to listen.

Eleanor Alder is a postgraduate student studying an English Masters at the University of Worcester. She has just completed her undergraduate degree at the university, in which she studied English Literature and Creative writing. This is her debut release.

RELEASED BY DARK THIRTY POETRY

ANTHOLOGY ONE
THIS ISN'T WHY WE'RE HERE
MORTAL BEINGS
POEMS THAT WERE WRITTEN ON TRAINS
BUT WEREN'T WRITTEN ABOUT TRAINS
CLOSING SHIFT DREAMS
DESIRE
ANIMATE
THESEUS AND I

Printed in Great Britain
by Amazon

19497648R00031